Superhero Powers
I am a Superhero!

Written by Jenna Bayne

Balboa Press books may be ordered through booksellers or by contacting:

Balboa Press
A Division of Hay House
1663 Liberty Drive
Bloomington, IN 47403
www.balboapress.com
1 (877) 407-4847

ISBN: 978-1-5043-8659-3 (sc)
ISBN: 978-1-5043-8660-9 (e)

Library of Congress Control Number: 2017912976

Print information available on the last page.

Balboa Press rev. date: 08/24/2017

BALBOA
PRESS
A DIVISION OF HAY HOUSE

Dedication

This book is dedicated to someone I have looked up to my entire life. He has been my proudest supporter, my biggest challenger and my dearest friend.

This book is dedicated to my Superhero brother, Jordan.

I love you more than you will ever know.

"I cannot fight the fight for you. But, I will always be your corner man" - JB

A Message from The Author

Dear Fellow Superhero,

It is with great honor to have you here. The contents of this book hold the most precious information, and once you possess this knowledge your life will forever be changed. Reciting the words of *Superhero Powers* will unlock the superhero powers that exist in you. These powers are given to you for a purpose, and just like Spider-man learned, "with great power comes great responsibility". The world chose you Superhero. You have a mission on this earth, are you willing and ready to accept it?

As you move forward with this knowledge, that you are a Superhero, and look for the powers that you possess, remember two very important secrets I will reveal to you now. The first secret is that your superpowers already exist within you. All you have to do is be who you are.

It is in my own opinion that the study of neuroscience is the most interesting science out there because each of our minds is so different. How we think, what we like, why we do what we do is all motivated by different neural pathways and interpretations. Our brain structure is similar to each other but the wiring of our minds is what makes us unique. How cool is that? Your unique brain is the most precious superpower of all, and where all your powers are born. Do not forget to value your uniqueness, honor your visions, act on your desires and make a positive impact on this world. This is the first step to being the world's greatest Superhero.

The second important secret to being a Superhero is to stay fully alert in each moment. Being a Superhero is really about noticing things. Noticing opportunities to use your powers to better the world. Noticing ways to treat yourself and others with love, compassion, and kindness. Being alert in the moment allows for you to be ready to quickly take action so you never miss out. I have said it before and I will say it again, the world needs you. You would not be here if this was not the case. Believe in yourself, stay present and act on your powerful responsibility as a Superhero.

Lastly, your superpowers are yours to discover. Anything that interests you, brings you joy or comes naturally to you, that does not inflict harm on you or others, is a superpower. Stay open, experience things, jump at opportunities and discover your inner superpowers. Your powers will grow, change and expand as you live your life. You are not in competition with others because you are the only **you** who exists in this universe. You can be, do and have anything that you want.

As Ollivander says to Harry in *Harry Potter and the Sorcerer's Stone* by J.K. Rowling, "The wand chooses the wizard, Harry...I think we must expect great things from you". Follow your inner desires and live your *Superhero Powers*, and I know we can expect great things from YOU.

Are you ready to live as a Superhero?

Mission accepted.

With deepest admiration,
Jenna

A Message to all Influencers of Children

Welcome to the BayneBooks® Series!

I'm thrilled that you have found the BayneBooks® Series to help you have an even greater impact on children. The BayneBooks® Series are personal development tools intended to be used daily to expose children to their innate magnificence. Each book represents one concept that aids in this mission by supporting the neurological development of young minds to establish healthy foundations of positive self-esteem and confidence. In other words, the BayneBooks® Series are tangible, leadership-strategy books disguised as entertaining children's books. They are meant to bond you with the children in your life, while positively impacting both of you. There are helpful companion tools such as games, worksheets and exercises that go along with each of the books. For access to these impactful materials check out jennabayne.com

Superhero Powers is just one of the many strategy books found in the BayneBooks® Series. The concept of this book is to teach our youth that they matter! Each child is so special, and it is vital that we fully immerse them into this idea. It is our job, as influencers of children, to guide children to live as the Superhero they were innately born to be. We need to allow them to follow their deepest interests and passions because it is these unique skills and talents that make up who they are. For more resources and ideas for teaching and learning about *Superhero Powers* check-out jennabayne.com

With enough passion, and practice every child can become, do and have anything that they want. With enough desire any behavior or any skill can be learned.

Having said that, we don't all need to become experts in the same thing. We all have our own unique life experiences, influences, genetic bio-individuality, and interests that lead us down different discoveries, passions and life courses. This is why encouraging children to own their own superpowers is so important. All superpowers are equally important and part of the evolution of our world.

Working with numbers, playing a musical instrument, dancing, creating art projects, being kind towards others, cooking, baking - the list goes on - whatever it is that makes your children thrive are their *Superhero Powers*. What they love and find enjoyable may not seem to be of much value right away, and this is okay. It is not our job to decide what they want; it is our job to discover with them and believe in them. As an influencer of children, this is one of our greatest superpowers.

Think of great artists, athletes and inventers. Take Michael Jordan's journey for an example. He is the most successful and talented NBA player in the world. He did not make the varsity basketball team. He was told he wasn't tall enough but he had ambition and great people in his life to encourage him. Everyone who has ever achieved something great did it because someone in their life challenged them too. Influencers of children often forget just how powerful we are. One simple sentence, a single demonstration of belief, one hour of quality time can catapult a life forward and positively change it forever. Superhero Influencers create Next Generational Superheroes.

Again, you have the power. You are the model and foundation for our future generations. Who do you want to be for your child? Remember that being you is the most impactful Superhero Power you could ever demonstrate.

This book is a gift for YOU
BECAUSE YOU ROCK!

Dear_____,

The message in this book
is one that makes me think of you.
You make this world a better place
because of all the things you do.

There are strengths that you have
that make you, uniquely, you.
You are a Superhero!
And this, I know to be true.

So, remember that your gifts
are really your superpower traits,
and when you use your powers wisely
you make our world great!

One of my favorite superpowers about you is:

_____

BE YOU!

Yours truly,

Superhero Powers
I am a Superhero!

If I was asked, "Who is a Superhero?"
this is what I would say.
I would say, "I am a Superhero
each and every day!"

Superheroes make people smile
and help those who need a hand.
They ask a lot of questions
to seek first to understand.

They often make mis-takes
when they are learning something new.
Superpowers need to be practiced,
so this is what Superheroes do.

I am a Superhero
because this is true for me!
I always strive to do my best
and be the best me I can be!

Superheroes are always learning
and love to cuddle up in bed.
They read all types of books
to keep their wise minds fed.

Superheroes sometimes feel excited
and sometimes they get mad.
Sometimes they feel happy,
and other moments they feel sad.

Sometimes Superheroes forget
and sometimes they wonder, "Why?"
But, a Superhero never says, "I can't"
because they always give another try.

Superheroes open doors for others
and say, "Thank you" and "Yes, please".
They are always looking for ways
to help those in need.

Spreading love and kindness
is a superpower trait.
Staying present in the moment
makes a Superhero great!

I am a Superhero
because this is true for me!
I always strive to do my best
and be the best me I can be!

So, what are my superpowers?
What makes me, me?
The possibilities are endless
for who it is that I can be.

My most precious superpower
already exists within me.
My mind is my superpower
where all my powers come to be.

By doing what I love,
I make this world a better place.
There is no one else quite like me
I cannot be replaced!

As long as I add value
and make me proud of me.
I know I will impact this world
and leave a legacy.

I accept my life mission
to be the best superhero I can be.
I am here to make an impact
to the largest degree.

I repeat this rhyme daily
as I do my Superhero stance.
I yell it from my heart
as I do my Superhero dance!

I AM A SUPERHERO
BECAUSE THIS IS TRUE FOR ME!
I ALWAYS STRIVE TO DO MY BEST
AND BE THE BEST ME I CAN BE!

Superhero Powers
I am a Superhero!

Extra, Extra!
There is so much more to discover!

Grab your cuddle buddy and head to jennabayne.com to download complementary and fun companion materials to go deeper with your superpowers.

You will:

- Discover YOUR superpowers
- Learn what others think your superpowers are
- Learn ways to teach others how to find their powers too
- Hear directly from the author
- And so much more!

JOIN THE

52/5
CHALLENGE

52 WEEKS
OF 5 MINUTE
CHALLENGES

THAT WILL EQUIP YOU
WITH THE STRATEGIES AND TECHNIQUES

TO L♥VE THE PEOPLE
IN YOUR LIFE BETTER.

BEGIN THE CHALLENGE AT
JENNABAYNE.COM/525

About the Author

Jenna Bayne is the size of a mouse but has the heart of a lion. She began as a classroom teacher in Ontario, Canada, while building her own virtual coaching practice dealing with disordered eating habits among teens and adults. Through her exposure working with young adults, she quickly identified a series of self-limiting challenges that continued to be brought to their one on one coaching sessions. From this insight and her deep understanding of how to support the educational system, she recognized the need for tangible resources to address and help to overcome these self-limiting beliefs at younger ages. Thus, BayneBooks® Series was born. Find out more about her nutritional courses, BayneBooks® companion materials and all other things Jenna at jennabayne.com.

CPSIA information can be obtained
at www.ICGtesting.com
Printed in the USA
BVHW02s1713070718
521006BV00011B/69/P

9 781504 386593